LET'S LEARN ABOUT NATURAL RESOURCES

FERTILE LAND AND SOIL

Jill Sherman

Enslow Publishing
101 W. 23rd Street
Suite 240
New York, NY 10011
USA
enslow.com

WORDS TO KNOW

antibiotics Medicines that kill bacteria.

atmosphere The gases that surround Earth.

carbon One of the elements needed for life.

fertile Having the power to give life and help growth.

microbes Tiny living things that can only be seen with a microscope. Some examples are bacteria, algae, and fungi.

natural resource Something from nature that people use.

nutrients Substances in food and soil that living things need to live and grow.

organic matter Decaying plants and animals.

CONTENTS

More than Dirt

Feel the earth beneath your feet. It's not just dirt. Look close and you see it also has clay and organic matter. You've got soil! Soil is one of Earth's most important natural resources.

Fertile Land

Earth is covered mostly by water. The rest is land. Some land is desert. Some is covered in ice. Other parts we build on and plant on. Fertile land is important to life. It has healthy soil.

Fast Fact

Rocks break down. Plants and animals decay. And soil is made. It takes thousands of years for Earth to produce just one inch of soil.

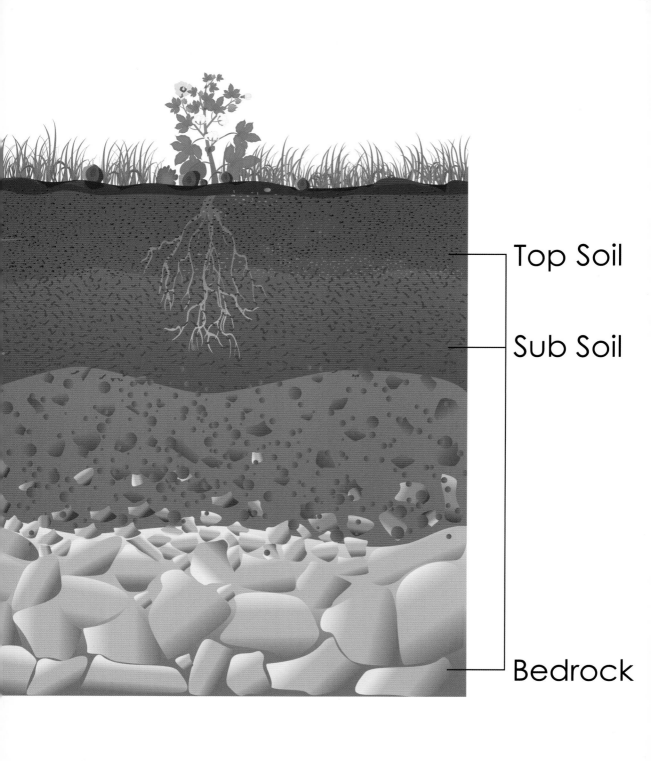

Top Soil

Sub Soil

Bedrock

A Home for Life

The crumbly top layer of land is soil. Without soil there would be no life. Worms and microbes in soil break down plant and animal life. They give soil important nutrients.

FAST FACT
There are three layers of soil: topsoil, subsoil, and bedrock.

Growing Things

Much of our food grows from Earth's soil. Water soaks into the soil like a sponge. As the plant roots absorb water, they also take in nutrients. Later, we absorb these nutrients when we eat the plants.

FAST FACT
Healthy soil soaks up lots of water to prevent floods.

Animals and Soil

Insects like ants and centipedes live in the soil. So do larger animals like moles and prairie dogs. They burrow into the earth, making the soil their homes.

Make It with Soil

When people want to create things, they look for materials from the world around them. Soil can come in many colors. We grind it up to mix into paint. Clay can be shaped. When it's baked we can make beautiful pottery.

FAST FACT
The oldest known pottery was uncovered in China. It dates back 20,000 years.

Building with Soil

We know that many animals build their homes in soil. But humans build with the earth as well. Dried mud and clay mixtures make sturdy building materials. Today's bricks, plaster, concrete, and glass are made with materials from the soil.

FAST FACT
Many homes in the American Southwest are made from adobe, a kind of mud brick.

Climate Control

Carbon is an important element to life on Earth. But too much carbon dioxide gas in our air is a problem. This gas traps heat in the atmosphere. Healthy soil can hold onto some of the carbon and keep it out of the air. This helps control Earth's climate.

Fast Fact
As temperatures rise, more carbon may be released from the soil into the air.

Soil Pollution

Like other natural resources, soil can be polluted. When too many chemicals go into the soil, it becomes unhealthy. Food grown in polluted soil can make people sick. Use care with chemicals so they don't end up where they don't belong.

FAST FACT
About 37 percent of Earth's total land can be used for farming.

Activity

SORTING SOIL

Procedure:

MATERIALS
garden soil
soda bottle
funnel
water

1. Fill the bottle most of the way with clean water.

2. Use the funnel to add soil to the bottle.

3. Screw on the cap and shake up the mixture.

4. Set the bottle down and watch the soil begin to settle.

5. Let it sit for 10 minutes and check again.

6. Observe several layers of sediment. Note the size of the particles in each layer. This is a process similar to how scientists analyze soil samples.

LEARN MORE

Books

Graham, Ian. *You Wouldn't Want to Live Without Dirt!* New York, NY: Franklin Watts, 2016.

MacAulay, Kelley. *Why Do We Need Soil?* New York, NY: Crabtree Publishing, 2014.

Tomeck, Steve. *Dirtmeister's Nitty Gritty Planet Earth.* New York, NY: National Geographic Kids, 2015.

Websites

Dig Deeper
soils4kids.org
The Soil Society of America shares educational resources for students about soil, its role in our communities, career exploration, and experiments.

Time for Kids: Celebrate Earth Day
timeforkids.com / minisite / celebrate-earth-day
Explore a variety of ways that you can help protect Earth's natural resources. Enjoy fun Earth Day activities that you can do any day of the year!

INDEX

Published in 2018 by Enslow Publishing, LLC.
101 W. 23rd Street, Suite 240, New York, NY 10011

Copyright © 2018 by Enslow Publishing, LLC.

All rights reserved.

No part of this book may be reproduced by any means without the written permission of the publisher.

Library of Congress Cataloging-in-Publication Data

Names: Sherman, Jill, author.
Title: Fertile land and soil / Jill Sherman.
Description: New York : Enslow Publishing, 2018. | Series: Let's learn about natural resources | Includes bibliographical references and index. |
Audience: Grades K to 3.
Identifiers: LCCN 2017011016| ISBN 9780766091412 (library bound) | ISBN 9780766091399 (pbk.) | ISBN 9780766091405 (6 pack)
Subjects: LCSH: Soils—Juvenile literature.
Classification: LCC S591.3 .S54 2017 | DDC 631.4—dc23
LC record available at https://lccn.loc.gov/2017011016

Printed in China

To Our Readers: We have done our best to make sure all website addresses in this book were active and appropriate when we went to press. However, the author and the publisher have no control over and assume no liability for the material available on those websites or on any websites they may link to. Any comments or suggestions can be sent by email to customerservice@enslow.com.

Photo Credits: Cover, p. 1 Jochen Schlenker/Publisher Mix/Getty Images; interior pages (soil, grass, sky) Andrey_Kuzmin/Shutterstock.com; interior pages (sign) johavel/Shutterstock.com; p. 4 lorenzo gambaro/Shutterstock.com; p. 6 Yusnizam Yusof/Shutterstock.com; p. 8 snapgalleria/Shutterstock.com; p. 10 Annaev/Shutterstock.com; p. 12 Michael C. Gray/Shutterstock.com; p. 14 Kokhanchikov/Shutterstock.com, (inset) Grisha Bruev/Shutterstock.com; p. 16 Irina Smirnova/Shutterstock.com; p. 18 Carlos Caetano/Shutterstock.com; p. 20 Sergiy Bykhunenko/Shutterstock.com.